Ralph Masiello's FAIRY DRAWING BOOK

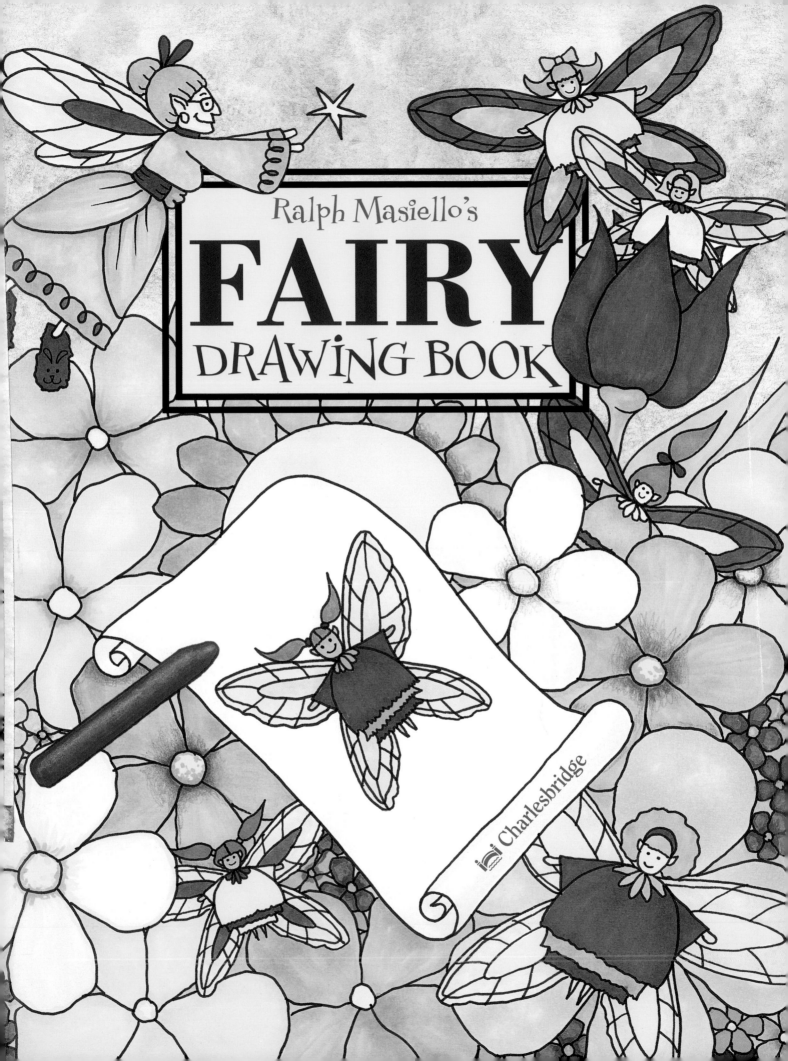

Charlesbridge

For Julia, Marina, Ava, and Kendall. And especially for my daughter, Talia, who has asked me over and over since she was three years old to do a fairy book. Here it is!

Also in this series:

Ralph Masiello's Ancient Egypt Drawing Book

Ralph Masiello's Bug Drawing Book

Ralph Masiello's Dinosaur Drawing Book

Ralph Masiello's Dragon Drawing Book

Ralph Masiello's Farm Drawing Book

Ralph Masiello's Halloween Drawing Book

Ralph Masiello's Ocean Drawing Book

Ralph Masiello's Robot Drawing Book

Other books illustrated by Ralph Masiello:

The Dinosaur Alphabet Book

The Extinct Alphabet Book

The Flag We Love

The Frog Alphabet Book

The Icky Bug Alphabet Book

The Icky Bug Counting Book

The Mystic Phyles: Beasts

The Skull Alphabet Book

The Yucky Reptile Alphabet Book

Cuenta los insectos

Copyright © 2013 by Ralph Masiello

Published by Charlesbridge
85 Main Street
Watertown, MA 02472
(617) 926-0329
www.charlesbridge.com

Library of Congress Cataloging-in-Publication Data
Masiello, Ralph.
 Ralph Masiello's fairy drawing book / Ralph Masiello.
  p. cm.
 ISBN 978-1-57091-539-0 (reinforced for library use)
 ISBN 978-1-57091-540-6 (softcover)
 ISBN 978-1-60734-655-5 (ebook)
1. Fairies in art—Juvenile literature. 2. Drawing—Technique—Juvenile literature.
I. Title. II. Title: Fairy drawing book.
NC825.F22M37 2013
743'.87—dc23   2012011315

Printed in China
(hc) 10 9 8 7 6 5 4 3 2 1
(sc) 10 9 8 7 6 5 4 3 2 1

Illustrations done in mixed media
Display type set in Couchlover, designed by Chank, Minneapolis, Minnesota;
 text type set in Goudy
Color separations by KHL Chroma Graphics, Singapore
Printed and bound November 2012 by Jade Productions in Heyuan, Guangdong, China
Production supervision by Brian G. Walker
Designed by Susan Mallory Sherman and Whitney Leader-Picone

Greetings, Artistic Fairy Fans.

When my youngest daughter was little, she shared with me her fascination with fairies. Together we read fairy books, drew these miniature beings, and tried to find flying friends wherever we went. We even left tiny treats for fairy visitors at the foot of the pine trees in our backyard.

In this book I hope to share my daughter's enchantment with fairies by showing you some simple ways to draw your own. You might even recognize a few famous wand-holding fairies as you learn to illustrate a variety of winged creatures.

Follow the steps in red to create your drawings. Then color in your artwork with your favorite tools. Try the extra challenge steps in blue to add even more fun and fantasy to your art.

Have fun!

Ralph

Choose your tools

pastel pencil crayon watercolor fine-tip marker colored pencil marker poster paint

Ballet Fairy

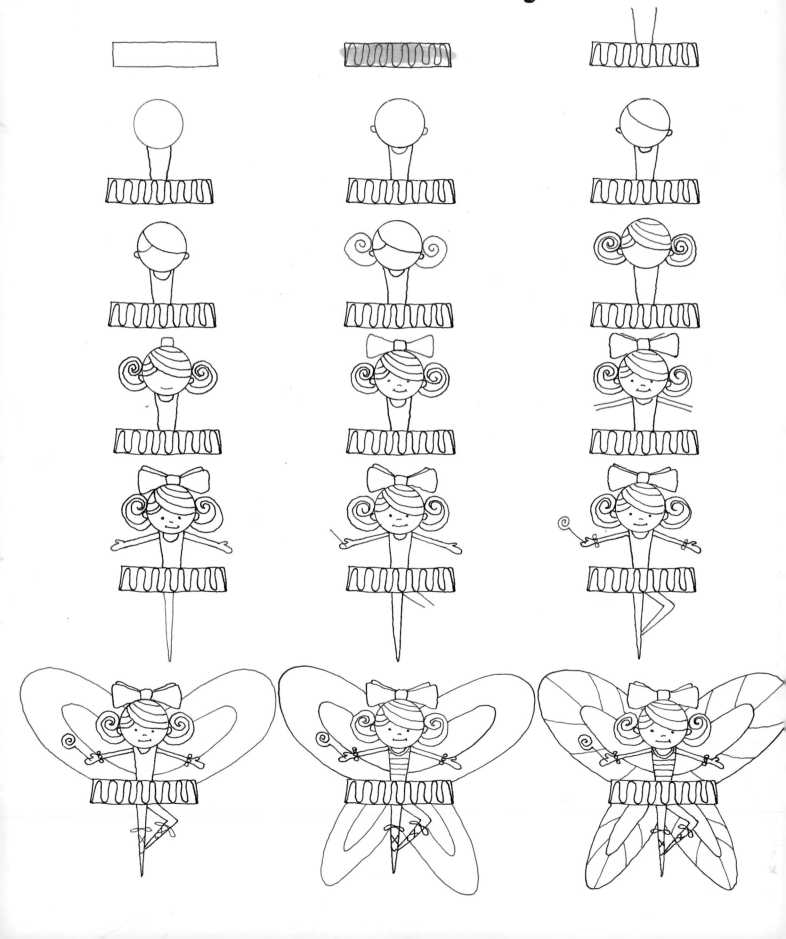

Dance, prance, and fly away.

crayon and marker

Dewdrop Fairy

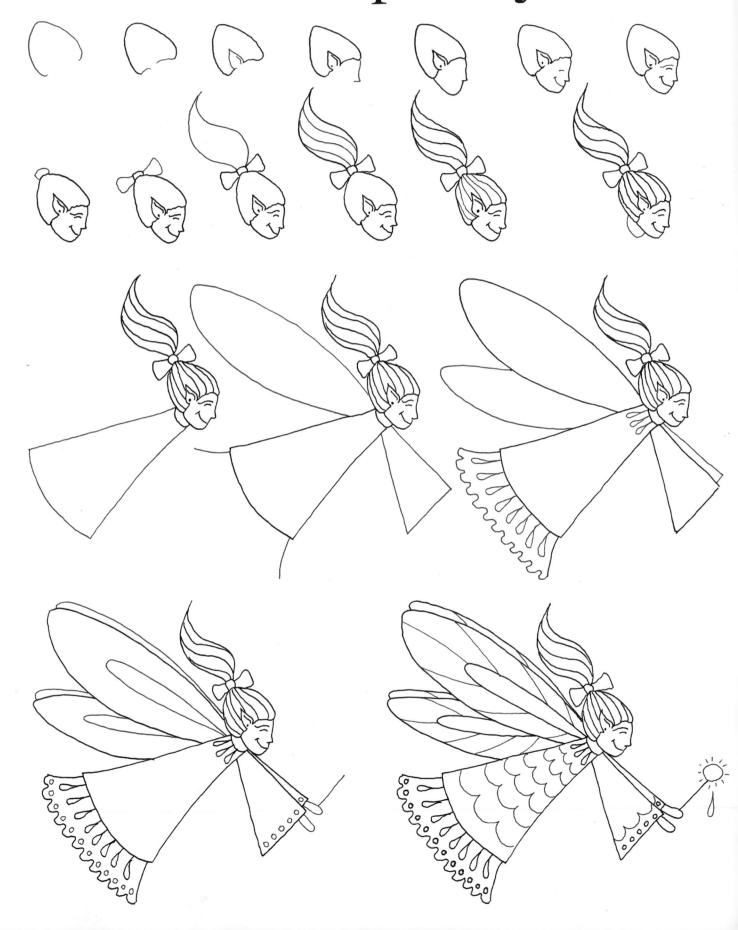

Oh, dew I love to draw!

marker

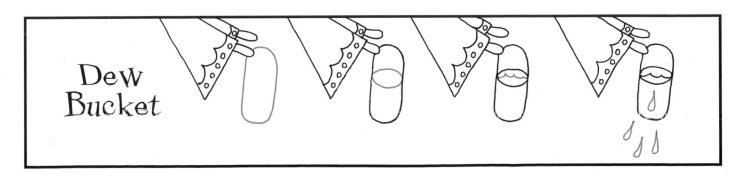

Dew
Bucket

Rainbow Fairy

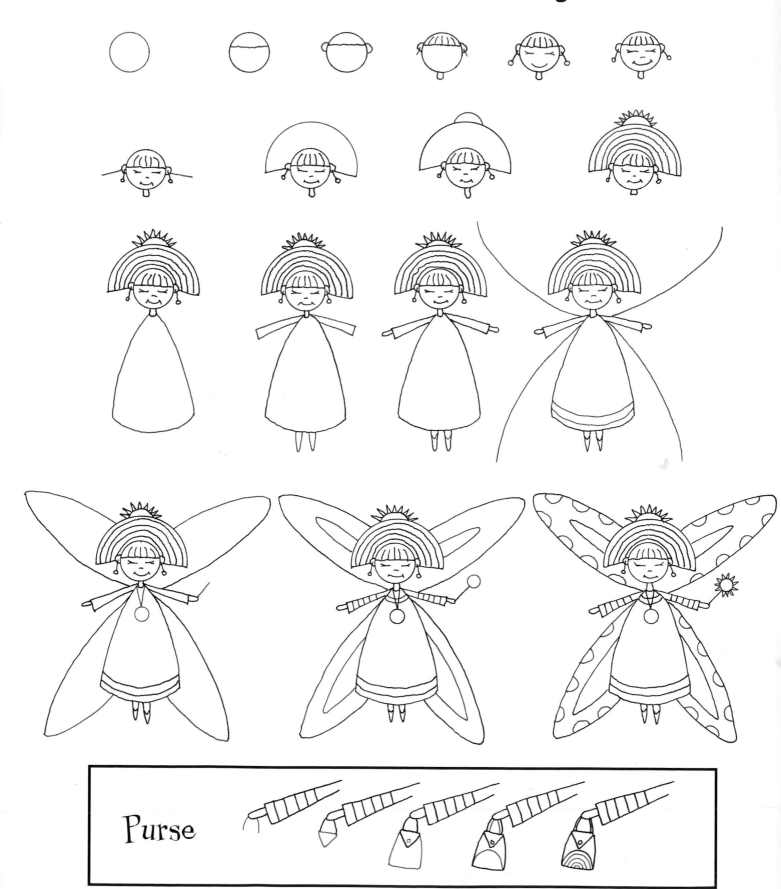

Purse

Color your way over the rainbow.

colored pencil and watercolor

Garden Fairy

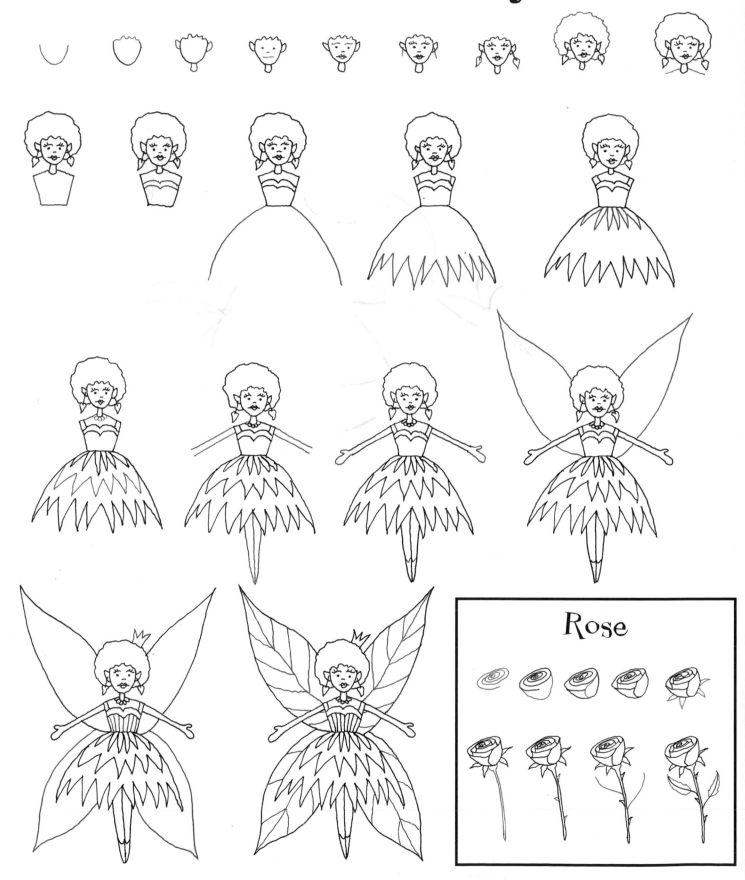

Rose

My work is a bed of roses.

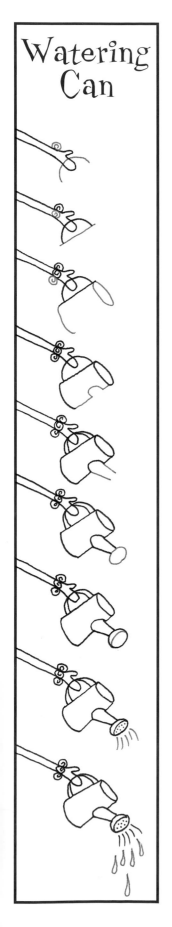

marker and pastel pencil

Heart Fairy

Put more heart into your art!

marker and crayon

Tiny Fairy

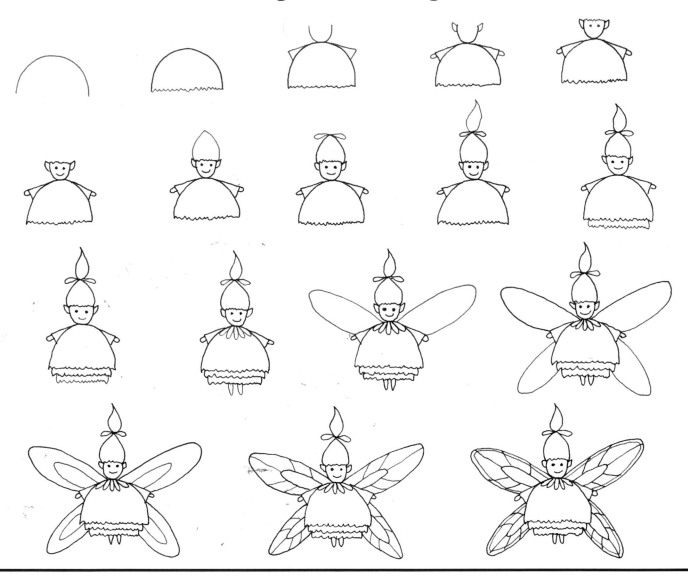

Fairy Hairstyles

Star

Moon

Take flight on a moonlit night.

watercolor, marker, pastel pencil, and poster paint

Hairy Fairy

A fairy can be quite hairy!

marker and pastel pencil

Brush and Mirror

Tooth Fairy

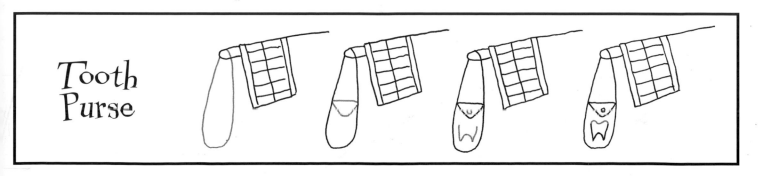

Tooth
Purse

Fairy Godmother

Flowers

Sugarplum Fairy

Wrapped Candy   Candy Cane

Famous fairies flutter about.

watercolor, marker, and crayon

Princess Fairy

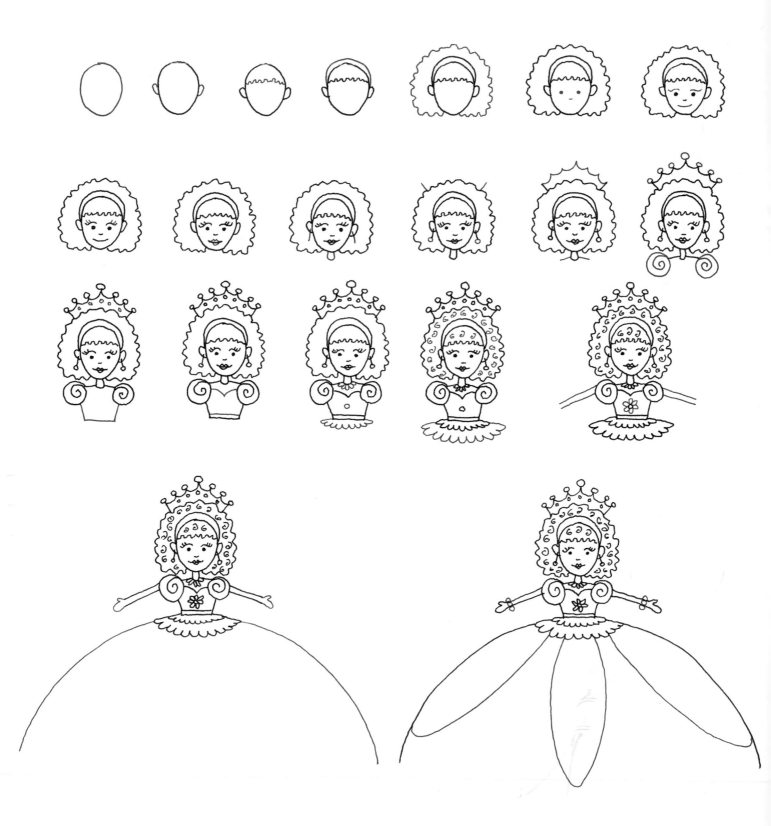

A royal masterpiece.

marker and colored pencil

Fashion a family
of fanciful fairies!

Resources

Books

Andrews, Julie, and Emma Walton Hamilton. *The Very Fairy Princess*. New York: Little, Brown, 2010.
Geraldine proves that being a real fairy princess means letting your sparkle out, taking charge, and much more.

Barker, Cicely Mary. *How to Find Flower Fairies*. New York: Penguin, 2007.
A scrapbook of pop-up fairy homes shares mysterious secrets about fairy life.

Kane, Tracy L. *Fairy Houses*. Lee, NH: Light-Beams, 2001.
Kristen builds a fairy house in the woods and patiently waits for fairies to come visit.

Kane, Barry, and Tracy Kane. *Fairy Houses . . . Everywhere!* Lee, NH: Light-Beams, 2006.
A photographic celebration of seasonal fairy houses made from natural materials.

Moorey, Teresa. *The Fairy Bible: The Definitive Guide to the World of Fairies*. New York: Sterling, 2008.
A handbook about fairy existence details the foods fairies prefer, the plants they treasure, and the animals they adore.

Shannon, David. *Alice the Fairy*. New York: Blue Sky, 2004.
Alice hasn't learned all the tricks of what it means to be a real fairy, but she knows a thing or two about everyday magic.

Websites

Disney FamilyFun: Fairy Houses
http://familyfun.go.com/crafts/fairy-houses-667271/
Collect materials from the natural world, including bark, moss, shells, or pinecones, and build a cozy home for fairy friends.

Fairy Food Recipes
http://www.recipebridge.com/r/fairy-food-recipes
Make fairy bread or the cake of the Sugar Plum Fairy.

Groovy Kids Parties: It's a Fairy Party
http://www.groovy-kids-parties.com/fairyparty.html
Endless fairy games and party ideas for your next celebration.

Kids Corner: Curious Creatures—Fairies
http://www.iofm.net/kidscorner/creatures/fairies.php
Discover a variety of named fairies—from brownies to gnomes to elves—and learn how to keep unwanted fairies away.

Rainbow Magic
http://www.rainbowmagiconline.com/uk/index.html
Enter a virtual world of weather fairies, rainbow fairies, magic animal fairies, and more. Design your own fairy and complete word searches and downloadable activities.